COCKTAILS

COCKTAILS

Oona van den Berg

HERMES
HOUSE

This paperback edition published by Hermes House
an imprint of
Anness Publishing Limited
Hermes House
88-89 Blackfriars Road
London SE1 8HA

A CIP catalogue record for this book is available from the British Library

Publisher: Joanna Lorenz
Editor: Sarah Ainley
Designer: Simon Wilder
Photographer: Steve Baxter
Stylist: Judy Williams

PHOTOGRAPHIC CREDIT
Many thanks to Fiskars UK Ltd for the use of their range of Kitchen Devils
knives and chopping boards, to Magimix for the use of the Professional
blender and Privilege food processor and to DuPont for the loan of the
Berndes Signocast saucepans.

MEASURES
Three sets of equivalent measures have been provided in these recipes,
in the following order: bar measures, metric and imperial. It is essential
that units of measurements are not mixed within each recipe. Where
conversions result in awkward numbers, these have been rounded for
convenience, but are accurate enough to produce successful results.
Note: 1 measure = $1/6$ of a gill = 22.5 ml

© Anness Publishing Limited 1998
Updated © 2000
10 9 8 7 6 5 4 3 2 1

CONTENTS

INTRODUCTION

The true origin of the first cocktails is not certain, but without doubt it was in America that these "mixed drinks" gained their popularity and where many of the more recent favourites were concocted. Cocktails developed in America with bourbon, Southern Comfort and Canadian rye whisky vying for attention. Prohibition was intended to curb drinking habits but resulted in people ingeniously distilling their own spirits, which were softened by the addition of mixers.

From the 1930s the cocktail truly took off. Chic and classic with a strong American twist, the Harvey Wallbanger, the Martini and the Manhattan are here to stay, but more recently, flamboyant tropical cocktails have proved popular. Coconut milk and fruits are whizzed together to create long frothy drinks: these concoctions are easily recreated at home now that exotic ingredients are readily available from the larger supermarkets.

Traditionally, a cocktail is made from no more than two spirits or liqueurs and the bartender's worth is gauged by making them with just enough zing, shaken or stirred to taste.

As a general rule, the simpler cocktails and those that are served clear, are just stirred over ice, in a bar glass, before being strained into a serving glass. Drinks that contain fizzy liquids are never shaken, for the obvious, explosive reasons. Cocktails with large quantities of fruit juices, syrups or eggs are shaken over ice in a cocktail shaker; cocktails containing milk, cream, ice cream or coconut milk make wonderful, frothy drinks when whizzed in a blender.

"Bar speak" is something to get acquainted with: a recipe suggesting a "dash of bitters" means just a shake of the bottle, while a "squeeze of lemon rind" does not mean the whole fruit floating in the drink. The rind should be held over the glass and twisted in the fingers, so that the lemon oils drop into the cocktail; it is then discarded. "On the rocks" simply means served over ice and "straight up" means the drink served as it is, in a chilled glass.

At home you can create cocktails with no more than a cocktail shaker, large pitcher, blender and a few essential ingredients such as bitters, plain sugar syrup and, of course, a couple of bottles of your favourite spirits and liqueurs. Making cocktails is an enjoyable pastime, so stir up a drink, sit back and savour!

GLASSES

Glasses should always be washed and dried with a glass cloth to ensure they are sparkling clean. Many recipes suggest chilled glasses but don't be tempted to put the best crystal in the freezer; leaving glasses at the back of the fridge works just as well.

COCKTAIL OR MARTINI GLASSES Classic and elegant, this glass is a wide conical bowl on a tall stem, to keep warm hands away from the drink. It holds about 150 ml/¼ pint/⅔ cup.

COLLINS GLASS The tallest of the tumblers, narrow with straight sides, it holds about 300 ml/½ pint/1¼ cups and is used for long drinks made with fresh juices or topped up with soda.

OLD-FASHIONED GLASS Classic shorts (whisky) tumblers are used for shorter drinks served "on the rocks". They hold about 175 ml/6 fl oz/¾ cup.

HIGHBALL GLASS The middle-sized tumbler and the most used. It holds about 250 ml/8 fl oz/1 cup.

LIQUEUR GLASS A glass for small measures of about 50 ml/2 fl oz/¼ cup.

BRANDY BALLOON OR SNIFTER This glass has been designed to trap the fragrance of the brandy in the bowl of the glass. The cocktail is further helped by being cupped in the palms of the hands to warm it gently and release the aroma.

LARGE COCKTAIL GOBLETS These are used for serving long frothy drinks. The wide rims of the glasses leave room for flamboyant decoration.

CHAMPAGNE GLASSES Champagne can be served from either attractive old-fashioned bowls or tall, slim flutes. The flute is the more efficient at conserving the fizz and the bubbles.

RED WINE BALLOON A useful size of wine glass, holding about 300 ml/½ pint/1¼ cups. These glasses are only filled to half capacity, to allow the wine to be swirled around inside.

WHITE WINE GLASS This is a long-stemmed medium-size glass that, once again, is good for keeping warm hands away from the chilled wine or cocktail.

POUSSE-CAFÉ A thin and narrow glass that stands on a short stem. The pousse-café is used for floating or layering stronger liqueur cocktails.

1 cocktail glass
2 Collins glass
3 old-fashioned glass
4 highball glass
5 liqueur glass
6 brandy balloon
7 large cocktail goblet
8 champagne flute
9 champagne bowl
10 red wine balloon
11 white wine glass
12 pousse-café

COCKTAIL EQUIPMENT

To make a successful cocktail you will need a few essential pieces of bartender's equipment. The most vital and flamboyant of these is the cocktail shaker; what you have in the cupboard can be substituted for the rest. The equipment listed below is in descending order of importance.

COCKTAIL SHAKER For mixing cocktails made with juices and syrups that do not depend on being crystal clear. The three-piece shaker is the easiest to handle, with a base to hold ice and liquids and a built-in strainer in the top.

BLENDER Goblet blenders are the best shape for mixing or frothing cocktails, or for blending cocktails with ice.

1 blender
2 cocktail shakers
3 fruit juice press
4 wooden hammer
5 canelle knife
6 corkscrew
7 bar spoon
8 strainer
9 drinking straws
10 tot measures
11 measuring spoons
12 cup measures
13 cocktail sticks
14 swizzle stick
15 nutmeg grater
16 dish towel
17 sharp knife

ICE BAG OR DISH TOWEL Use to hold ice cubes when crushing. The ice bag and towel must always be clean.

WOODEN HAMMER Use to crush ice.

TOT MEASURES OR MEASURING JUG The measurements can be in single or double bar measures, fluid ounces or millilitres.

STRAINER For pouring drinks from the shaker or bar glass to a cocktail glass.

MIXING PITCHER OR BAR GLASS Use for mixing drinks that are not shaken. This method is for drinks that are meant to be clear, not cloudy.

CORKSCREW The fold-away type, with a can opener and bottle-top opener, is very useful to have to hand.

BAR SPOON These long-handled spoons are used for mixing the drink directly in the glass.

MUDDLER A long stick with a bulbous end, this is used for crushing sugar or mint leaves.

LEMON KNIFE AND SQUEEZER A sharp knife is required for cutting citrus fruits and a squeezer is used for extracting the juice.

NUTMEG GRATER A tiny grater with small holes for grating nutmeg over egg-nogs and frothy drinks.

STRAWS, SWIZZLE AND COCKTAIL STICKS Used for the finishing decorative touches that complete a cocktail.

ZESTER AND CANELLE KNIFE Use these more specialist pieces of equipment for presenting fruit when dressing cocktail glasses.

CRUSHING ICE

Some cocktails require cracked or crushed ice, or a finely crushed ice snow for blending. Do not do this in a blender or food processor as you may find it makes the blade blunt.

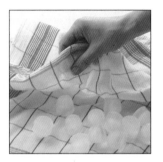

1 Lay a cloth on a work surface and cover half of the cloth with ice cubes. Alternatively, place the ice cubes in a cloth ice bag.

2 Fold the cloth over and, using the end of a rolling pin or a wooden hammer, strike the ice firmly, several times, until you achieve the required fineness.

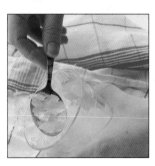

3 Spoon or scrape the fine ice snow into glasses or a pitcher. Fine ice snow must be used immediately, but cracked or crushed ice can be stored in the freezer in plastic bags.

DECORATIVE ICE CUBES

Decorative ice cubes can instantly jazz up even the simplest cocktails. Add flavour and colour to ice cubes with fruits, olives or leaves, and then freeze the ice as normal.

1 Fill each compartment of an ice cube tray half-full with water and place in the freezer for 2–3 hours or until the water has frozen.

2 Prepare the fruit, olives, mint leaves, lemon rind, raisins or borage flowers and dip each in water. Place in the ice cube trays and freeze again.

3 Top up the ice cube trays with water and return to the freezer to freeze completely. Use the ice cubes as required.

FROSTING GLASSES

Frosting adds to the look and taste of a cocktail. Use celery salt, grated coconut, grated chocolate, coloured sugars or cocoa for a similar effect. Chill the frosted glass in the fridge until needed.

1 Hold the glass upside-down, so the juice does not run down the glass. Rub the rim of the glass with the cut surface of a lemon, lime, orange or even a slice of fresh pineapple.

2 Keeping the glass upside-down, dip the rim into a shallow layer of sugar or salt. Re-dip the glass, if necessary, so that the rim is well coated.

3 Stand the glass upright and leave it until the salt or sugar has dried on the rim, then chill in the fridge.

SHAKING COCKTAILS

Cocktails that contain sugar syrups or creams require more than just a stir and are combined and chilled by briefly shaking together with ice. It is only possible to shake one or two servings at a time.

1 Fill the cocktail shaker two-thirds full with ice cubes and pour in the spirits. Add the mixers, if not sparkling, and the flavouring ingredients.

2 Put the lid on the shaker and hold it firmly, keeping the lid in place with one hand. Shake for about 10 seconds to blend simple concoctions and for 20–30 seconds for drinks with sugar syrups or eggs.

3 The outside of the shaker should now feel chilled. Remove the small lid and pour into the prepared glass. Use a strainer if the shaker is not already fitted with one.

BASIC SUGAR SYRUP

A sugar syrup is sometimes preferable to crystal sugars for sweetening cocktails, since it blends immediately with the other ingredients.

Makes about 750 ml/24 fl oz/3 cups

Ingredients
350 g/12 oz/1½ cups caster sugar
600 ml/20 fl oz/2½ cups water

1 Place the sugar in a heavy-based pan with the water, and heat gently over a low heat. Stir with a wooden spoon until the sugar has dissolved.

2 Brush the sides of the pan with a pastry brush dampened in water to remove any sugar crystals that might cause the sugar syrup to crystallize.

3 Bring to the boil for 3–5 minutes. Skim off any scum and, when no more appears, remove the pan from the heat. Cool the syrup and pour into clean, dry, airtight bottles. The syrup can be stored in the fridge for up to one month.

FLAVOURED SYRUPS

Syrup can be flavoured with any ingredient you like. Add to the basic syrup, bring to the boil, then bottle with the syrup.

Makes about 450 ml/15 fl oz/1⅞ cups

Ingredients
900 g/2 lb very ripe soft or stone fruit, washed
350 g/12 oz/1½ cups caster sugar

1 Place the washed fruit of your choice in a bowl. Using the bottom of a rolling pin, crush the fruit to release the juices. Cover and leave overnight to concentrate the flavour.

2 Strain through muslin, removing as much juice as possible. Measure the juice and add 225 g/8 oz/ 1 cup sugar per 300 ml/ ½ pint/1¼ cups fruit juice.

3 Place the pan over a low heat and stir until all the sugar has dissolved. Continue as in the recipe for basic sugar syrup. The syrup will keep in the fridge for up to one month.

Cook's Tip
Raspberries, black or redcurrants, plums and peaches will all make delicious flavoured syrups.

FLAVOURED SPIRITS

Gin, vodka and white rum can be left to steep and absorb the flavours of a wide variety of soft fruits.

Makes 1.2 litres/40 fl oz/5 cups

Ingredients
450 g/1 lb raspberries, strawberries, pineapple or sloes
225 g/8 oz/1 cup caster sugar
1 litre/35 fl oz/4 cups gin or vodka

1 Place the fruit in a wide-necked jar and add the sugar. If using sloes, prick them first with a needle or fine skewer, to release their flavour.

2 Add the spirit of your choice and cover the jar tightly. Store in a cool, dark place for about a month, shaking gently every week.

3 Strain through muslin and squeeze out the rest of the liquid from the steeped fruit. Return the flavoured spirit to a clean bottle, seal and store it in a cool, dark place.

Variations
Vodka and bananas; white rum and fresh pineapple; gin and drained, canned lychees, sliced peaches or apricots; brandy and plums or apricots.

STEEPING SPIRITS

Steeping a spirit with a strong flavouring ingredient, such as chillies, will give an interesting flavour.

Makes 1 litre/35 fl oz/4 cups

Ingredients
1 litre/35 fl oz/4 cups sherry or vodka
25–50 g/1–2 oz small red chillies, or to taste

1 Wash and dry the red chillies, discarding any that are less than perfect. Use a cocktail stick to prick the chillies all over, to release their flavour.

2 Tightly pack the chillies into a sterilized bottle.

3 Top up the bottle with sherry or vodka. Fit the cork tightly and leave in a cool, dark place for at least ten days or up to two months.

Variations
Gin with star anise or juniper berries; brandy with 15 g/ ½ oz/⅛ cup whole cloves; vodka with 50 g/2 oz/⅓ cup raisins or 15–30 ml/1–2 tbsp cracked black peppercorns.

SHORT & SHARP

GIBSON

This version of the Martini uses a pearl onion, rather than a lemon twist. You may prefer to use more gin.

Serves 1

Ingredients
½ measure/10 ml/2 tsp extra-dry vermouth
1 scant measure/20 ml/1¼ tbsp extra-dry gin
2 pearl onions, to decorate

1 Pour the vermouth over ice in a bar glass, stir well, then pour out. Use only the vermouth clinging to the ice and glass.

2 Add the gin and stir for at least 30 seconds, until the gin is well chilled.

3 Strain into a martini glass, either on the rocks or straight up.

4 Thread the pearl onions on to a cocktail stick and add to the drink.

Variation
With a touch more dry vermouth and a twist of lemon you will have an Australian Kangaroo.

EAST INDIA

This elegant drink can be served as an apéritif, with a twist of lime rind and a maraschino cherry.

Serves 1

Ingredients
⅔ measure/15 ml/1 tbsp brandy
2 dashes white curaçao
2 dashes pineapple juice
2 dashes angostura bitters
1 lime and a maraschino cherry, to decorate

1 Put the brandy, curaçao, pineapple juice and bitters into a bar glass half-filled with ice cubes.

2 Stir the cocktail well for 20 seconds until chilled, then strain into a tumbler over the rocks.

3 Using a canelle knife, remove a piece of rind from a lime.

4 Tightly twist into a coil, hold for 4 seconds, and add to the drink with a maraschino cherry.

Variation
Mix equal quantities of dry vermouth and dry sherry with angostura bitters, and serve on the rocks.

MARGARITA

This popular apéritif is made with tequila and Cointreau, but is also good with vodka and triple sec.

Serves 1

Ingredients
1 measure/22.5 ml/1½ tbsp tequila
1 measure/22.5 ml/1½ tbsp Cointreau
⅔ measure/15 ml/1 tbsp fresh lime juice
wedge of fresh lime, fine salt crystals and
whole cucumber, to decorate

1 Rub the rim of the glass with the lime, then invert the glass into salt. Turn the right way up and chill.

2 Add tequila, Cointreau, and lime juice to a cocktail shaker filled with ice. Shake for 20 seconds.

3 Carefully strain the cocktail into the prepared frosted glass.

4 Using a sharp knife, cut a strip of peel from the cucumber. Thread on to a cocktail stick and add to the glass, to decorate.

Variation
Replace Cointreau with blue curaçao for extra colour.

GIN SMASH

Use fresh peppermint, apple mint or black mint to produce three uniquely flavoured drinks.

Serves 1

Ingredients
15 ml/1 tbsp caster sugar
4 sprigs of fresh mint
2 measures/45 ml/3 tbsp dry gin

1 Dissolve the sugar in a little water in a cocktail shaker. Crush some ice.

2 Add mint to the shaker and press against the sides to extract the juices.

3 Half fill the shaker with the ice and add the gin. Replace the lid and shake for about 20 seconds, to mix the gin with the mint.

4 Strain the cocktail into a small wine glass filled with more of the crushed ice. Decorate with fresh mint sprigs, to serve.

Variation
Use Southern Comfort or bourbon in place of the gin.

GALL BRACER

Serve this smart drink on the rocks in a tumbler or in a cocktail glass, with a maraschino cherry.

Serves 1

Ingredients
2 dashes angostura bitters
2 dashes grenadine
2 measures/45 ml/3 tbsp whisky
rind of 1 lemon
maraschino cherry, to decorate

1 Half fill a bar glass with ice. Add the angostura bitters, grenadine and whisky. Stir well to chill.

2 Place some ice in a short tumbler and pour the cocktail over it.

3 Squeeze the oil and juices from the lemon rind into the cocktail. Discard the lemon rind.

4 Add a maraschino cherry to the cocktail, to decorate, if you like.

Variation
For a cocktail called a Gall Trembler substitute gin for the whisky and add more bitters.

GOLDEN START

A delicious and very drinkable mix of Galliano, orange, pineapple and coconut cream.

Serves 1

Ingredients
2 measures/45 ml/3 tbsp Galliano
1 measure/22.5 ml/1½ tbsp orange juice, chilled
1 measure/22.5 ml/1½ tbsp pineapple juice, chilled
1 measure/22.5 ml/1½ tbsp white or orange curaçao
1 measure/22.5 ml/1½ tbsp coconut cream
30 ml/2 tbsp pineapple juice, to decorate
25 g/1 oz/2 tbsp caster sugar, to decorate

1 Put the Galliano, fruit juices and curaçao in a blender and process.

2 Add the coconut cream and 15 ml/1 tbsp ice snow and process until smooth.

3 Rub the rim of the glass with pineapple juice and invert into a saucer of sugar, to frost the rim.

4 Pour the cocktail into the prepared frosted glass while still frothy.

Variation
Replace curaçao with crème de cacao for a tropical twist.

HOODED CLAW

Prune juice with Amaretto and Cointreau makes a delicious digestif, poured over fine ice snow.

Serves 4

Ingredients
5 measures/120 ml/4 fl oz prune juice
2 measures/45 ml/3 tbsp Amaretto
1 measure/22.5 ml/1½ tbsp Cointreau

1 Pour the prune juice, Amaretto and Cointreau together into a cocktail shaker half-filled with ice.

2 Shake the cocktail for about 20 seconds, until it is well chilled.

3 Loosely fill four small liqueur glasses with finely crushed ice snow.

4 Strain the drink into the glasses and serve with short drinking straws.

Variation
Mix 6 parts prune juice with 1 part elderflower cordial for a non-alcoholic version. Serve chilled, on the rocks.

The difference in weight or density of the liqueurs keeps this cocktail strictly separated in layers.

Serves 1

Ingredients

1 measure/22.5 ml/1½ tbsp Kahlúa
1 measure/22.5 ml/1½ tbsp Grand Marnier
1 measure/22.5 ml/1½ tbsp Bailey's Irish Cream

1 In a small shooter or pousse-café glass, pour a 2 cm/¾ in layer of Kahlúa.

2 Invert a cold teaspoon, just touching the surface of the Kahlúa and the side of the glass.

3 Slowly and carefully pour the Grand Marnier over the back of the teaspoon, to create a second layer.

4 Pour the Bailey's over the back of a second clean spoon for the final layer. This will form the middle layer, pushing the Grand Marnier to the top.

Variation

Create a similar effect with equal quantities of Bailey's, Kahlúa and vodka, layered in that order.

AIRSTRIKE

A variation on a Val d'Isère Shooter, similar in idea to the Italian Flaming Sambucca.

Serves 1

Ingredients
2 measures/45 ml/3 tbsp Galliano
1 measure/22.5 ml/1½ tbsp brandy
1 star anise

1 Put the Galliano and brandy in a saucepan and heat gently, until warm.

2 Carefully pour into a heat-resistant glass, standing on a small plate. Add the star anise.

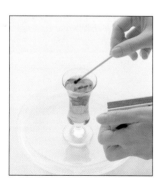

3 Using a long match, carefully pass the flame over the surface to ignite it. Leave to burn until the star anise has sizzled and released extra aroma into the drink. Leave to cool slightly before drinking. Take care as the top of the glass will be very hot.

Variation
Use only Sambucca and float 2–3 coffee beans on the surface instead of the star anise before lighting.

BRANDY BLAZER

A warming after-dinner tipple, ideal served with fresh vanilla ice cream or caramelized oranges.

Serves 1

Ingredients
½ orange
1 lemon
2 measures/45 ml/⅓ tbsp cognac
1 sugar cube
½ measure/10 ml/2 tsp Kahlúa
orange rind, threaded on to a cocktail stick, to decorate

1 Pare the rind from the fruits, removing and discarding as much of the white pith as possible.

2 Put the cognac, sugar cube, lemon and orange rind in a small saucepan.

3 Heat gently, then remove the pan from the heat, and pass a lighted match close to the surface of the liquid. Allow to burn for about 1 minute, then blow out.

4 Add the Kahlúa to the saucepan and strain into a heat-resistant liqueur glass. Decorate with the cocktail stick of orange rind. Serve warm.

BRANDY ALEXANDER

A warming digestif that can be served at
the end of the meal with coffee.

Serves 1

Ingredients
1 measure/22.5 ml/1½ tbsp brandy
1 measure/22.5 ml/1½ tbsp crème de cacao
1 measure/22.5 ml/1½ tbsp double (heavy) cream
whole nutmeg, to decorate

1 Half fill the cocktail
shaker with crushed ice,
then pour in the brandy,
crème de cacao and the
double (heavy) cream.

2 Shake vigorously for
about 20 seconds to mix
together well and to chill
the ingredients.

3 Strain the chilled cocktail into a small wine glass.

4 Grate a little nutmeg
over the top, to decorate.

Variation
Warm the brandy and cream gently in a saucepan,
then pour into a blender and add the crème de cacao.
Whizz until frothy. Serve with a cinnamon stick.

COOLERS & QUENCHERS

MORNING GLORY FIZZ

A good early-morning drink, to be consumed as soon as it is made, before it loses its bubbles.

Serves 1

Ingredients
⅔ measure/15 ml/1 tbsp brandy
¼ measure/5 ml/1 tsp orange curaçao
¼ measure/5 ml/1 tsp lemon juice
1 dash anisette
2 dashes angostura bitters
soda water, to taste
twist of lemon rind, to decorate

1 Pour the brandy, curaçao, lemon juice and anisette into a cocktail shaker containing ice and shake for 20 seconds.

2 Strain the drink into a small cocktail glass that has first been chilled in the fridge.

3 Add the angostura bitters to taste and top up the glass with soda water.

4 Using a canelle knife, cut a thin piece of lemon rind. Curl the rind into a tight coil and add it to the cocktail, to decorate.

TEQUILA SUNSET

A variation on the popular party drink which can be mixed in a pitcher, ready to pour into glasses.

Serves 1

Ingredients
1 measure/22.5 ml/1½ tbsp clear or golden tequila
5 measures/120 ml/4 fl oz lemon juice, chilled
1 measure/22.5 ml/1½ tbsp orange juice, chilled
15–30 ml/1–2 tbsp clear honey
⅔ measure/15 ml/1 tbsp crème de cassis

1 Pour the tequila and then the lemon and orange juices straight into a well-chilled cocktail glass.

2 Using a swizzle stick, mix the ingredients by twisting the stick between the palms of your hands.

3 Drizzle the honey into the centre of the cocktail. It will fall in a layer at the bottom of the glass.

4 Add the crème de cassis – but do not stir – to add a glowing layer above the honey in the glass.

Variation
To make a Tequila Sunrise, mix 2 parts tequila with 6 parts orange juice and 2 parts grenadine and stir.

GRASSHOPPER

If you use dark crème de cacao the cocktail will not be as vibrant but will taste just as good.

Serves 1

Ingredients
2 measures/45 ml/3 tbsp crème de menthe
2 measures/45 ml/3 tbsp light crème de cacao
2 measures/45 ml/3 tbsp double (heavy) cream
melted plain (bittersweet) chocolate, to decorate

1 Measure the crème de menthe and crème de cacao into a cocktail shaker and add the cream.

2 Add some cracked ice and shake well for about 20 seconds, until thoroughly mixed.

3 Strain the cocktail into a tumbler filled with finely cracked ice.

4 To decorate, spread the chocolate over a plastic board and leave to set. Using a sharp knife, draw the blade across the chocolate to create curls. Add to the top of the cocktail and serve.

COFFEE & CHOCOLATE FLIP

Drambuie can be used instead of brandy for a hint of honey, but don't add the sugar.

Serves 1

Ingredients
1 egg
5 ml/1 tsp caster sugar
1 measure/22.5 ml/1½ tbsp brandy
1 measure/22.5 ml/1½ tbsp Kahlúa
5 ml/1 tsp instant coffee granules
3 measures/70 ml/4½ tbsp double (heavy) cream
drinking chocolate powder or grated chocolate, to decorate

1 Separate the egg and lightly beat the egg white in a clean bowl until frothy.

2 In a separate bowl or glass, beat the egg yolk with the sugar.

3 In a small saucepan, gently warm together the brandy, Kahlúa, coffee granules and cream.

4 Let the cream mixture cool down, then whisk into the egg yolk. Add the egg white to the egg and cream and pour back and forth between two glasses, until the mixture is smooth.

5 Pour into a tall glass over coarsely crushed ice and sprinkle with chocolate powder or grated chocolate, to decorate.

MAI TAI

A very refreshing but strong party drink that slips down easily – just before you do!

Serves 1

Ingredients

1 measure/22.5 ml/1½ tbsp white (light) rum
1 measure/22.5 ml/1½ tbsp dark rum
1 measure/22.5 ml/1½ tbsp apricot brandy
3 measures/70 ml/4½ tbsp orange juice, chilled
3 measures/70 ml/4½ tbsp pineapple juice, chilled
1 measure/22.5 ml/1½ tbsp grenadine

1 Add the white (light) and dark rum and apricot brandy to a cocktail shaker half full of cracked ice.

2 Add the well-chilled orange and pineapple juices to the shaker.

3 Shake together well for about 20 seconds, or until the outside of the cocktail shaker feels cold. Strain into a tumbler of ice.

4 Slowly pour the grenadine into the glass and it will fall to the bottom of the drink to make a glowing red layer.

BLUE HAWAIIAN

This eye-catching drink can be decorated with a mixture of fruits and leaves.

Serves 1

Ingredients
1 measure/22.5 ml/1½ tbsp blue curaçao
1 measure/22.5 ml/1½ tbsp coconut cream
2 measures/45 ml/3 tbsp white (light) rum
2 measures/45 ml/3 tbsp pineapple juice
1 pineapple, 1 pear, 1 lime and 1 maraschino cherry, to decorate

1 Process the curaçao, coconut cream and white (light) rum in a blender until the colour is even.

2 Place ice cubes in a dish towel and crush to a fine snow with a rolling pin or wooden hammer.

3 Add the pineapple juice to the blender and process the mixture once more, until thick and frothy.

4 Spoon the crushed ice into a large cocktail glass and pour the cocktail over the ice.

5 Decorate the drink with pineapple leaves and a pineapple wedge, pear slices, a wedge of lime and a maraschino cherry. Serve with drinking straws.

Variation
For a Blue Lagoon, pour equal quantities of vodka and blue curaçao over ice and top up with lemonade.

CIDER CUP

This makes an excellent long and refreshing drink for an apéritif or party. Mix up just before serving.

Serves 6

Ingredients
rind of 1 lemon
slices of orange
5 measures/120 ml/4 fl oz pale sherry
3 measures/70 ml/4½ tbsp brandy or clove brandy
3 measures/70 ml/4½ tbsp white curaçao
2 measures/45 ml/3 tbsp Amaretto
600 ml/20 fl oz/2½ cups good quality medium-sweet cider
whole cucumber, to decorate

1 Partly fill a pitcher with cracked ice and add the fruit rind and slices.

2 Add the sherry, brandy, curaçao and Amaretto to the ice and stir well to mix.

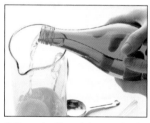

3 Pour in the cider and stir gently with a long swizzle stick, until well mixed.

4 Use a canelle knife to peel the cucumber in one piece, to form a spiral. Serve in chilled glasses, decorated with the fruit and cucumber peel.

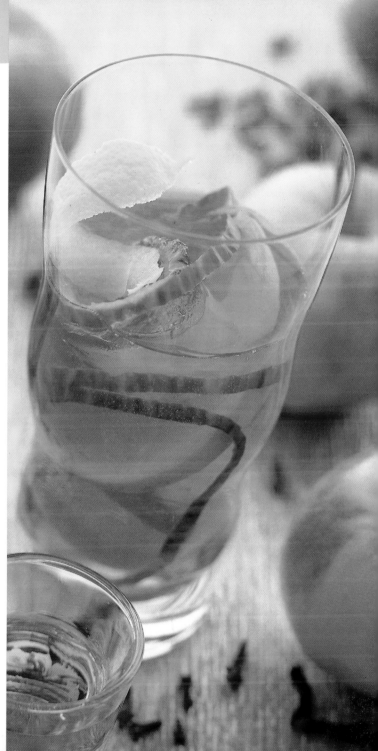

HAVANA COBBLER

An old-fashioned drink that is surprisingly refreshing served in hot weather.

Serves 1

Ingredients
5 ml/1 tsp sugar syrup
½ measure/10 ml/2 tsp green ginger wine
1 measure/22.5 ml/1½ tbsp Cuban or white (light) rum
1 measure/22.5 ml/1½ tbsp port

1 Put the sugar syrup and ginger wine in a cocktail shaker, half-filled with ice. Add the white (light) rum.

2 Shake together for 20 seconds, until the shaker feels cold on the outside.

3 Strain the cocktail into a chilled shorts (whisky) tumbler.

4 Tilt the glass and slowly pour the port down the side of the glass to form a layer floating on top.

Variation
Swap the rum for brandy, gin or sherry, or even wine or (omitting the port) champagne.

CRANBERRY KISS

A delicious cocktail, with the tang of cranberry and grapefruit and the sweetness of Marsala.

Serves 1

Ingredients

2 measures/45 ml/3 tbsp cranberry juice
2 measures/45 ml/3 tbsp pink grapefruit juice
1 measure/22.5 ml/1½ tbsp brandy
2 measures/45 ml/3 tbsp Marsala
redcurrant string, 1 egg white, lightly beaten,
and 15 g/½ oz/1 tbsp caster sugar,
to decorate

1 For the decoration, brush the redcurrants lightly with the egg white.

2 Shake caster sugar over the redcurrants, to cover them in a light frosting.

3 Place the fruit juices with the brandy in a cocktail shaker full of crushed ice and shake well to mix.

4 Strain the cocktail into a well-chilled glass. Tilt the glass slightly before slowly pouring the Marsala into the drink down the side.

5 Serve the cocktail decorated with the string of frosted redcurrants.

Variation

Shake the fruit juices with coconut milk and vodka or gin.

VUNDERFUL

A long, lazy Sunday afternoon tipple. Leave the fruits in the gin for as long as possible.

Serves 20

Ingredients
400g/14 oz can lychees
2 peaches, sliced
600 ml/20 fl oz/2½ cups gin
For each person:
1 measure/22.5 ml/1½ tbsp Pimms
2–3 dashes angostura bitters
5 measures/120 ml/4 fl oz chilled tonic water or lemonade
slice of lime, to decorate

1 Strain the lychees from the syrup and place them in a wide-necked jar with the peach slices and the gin. Leave overnight or for up to a month.

2 Per serving, mix in a large glass 1 measure/ 22.5 ml/1½ tbsp lychee gin with 1 measure/22.5 ml/ 1½ tbsp Pimms and add bitters to taste.

4 Add chilled tonic water or lemonade, to taste.

5 Put some of the drained gin-soaked lychees and peaches into each glass and add a muddler to stir and crush the fruit. Decorate with a lime slice.

3 Strain into tall tumblers filled with ice cubes.

MOSCOW MULE

A classic cocktail which uses angostura bitters for colour and enough vodka to give the drink a real kick.

Serves 1

Ingredients
2 measures/45 ml/3 tbsp vodka
6 dashes angostura bitters
dash lime cordial
½ measure/10 ml/½ tbsp fresh lime juice
3 measures/70 ml/4½ tbsp ginger beer
slices of lime, to decorate

1 Pour the vodka, bitters, lime cordial and lime juice into a bar glass of ice. Mix together well.

2 Strain the mixture into a tumbler containing a couple of ice cubes.

3 Top up the mixture, to taste, with ginger beer.

4 Add a few halved slices of lime, to serve.

Variation
For a Malawi Shandy, mix ice-cold ginger beer with a dash of bitters and top up with soda water. Of course, the vodka does not have to be left out.

NON-ALCOHOLIC

SCARLET LADY

This drink could fool a few on the first sip as an alcoholic wine-based cocktail.

Serves 1

Ingredients

115 g/4 oz Galia, honeydew or
watermelon
5 small red seedless grapes
3 measures/70 ml/4½ tbsp unsweetened
red grape juice
seedless grapes, 1 egg white, lightly beaten,
and 15 g/½ oz/1 tbsp caster sugar,
to decorate

1 Put the melon and grapes in a blender and process until they form a smooth purée.

2 Add the red grape juice to the blender and process for about another minute.

3 Strain the fruit juice into a bar glass filled with ice and stir until the juice is well chilled.

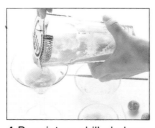

4 Pour into a chilled glass. For the decoration, dip the grapes in egg white and roll in caster sugar. Thread on to a cocktail stick.

SUNBURST

Bursting with freshness and vitamins, this drink makes a perfect early morning pick-me-up.

Serves 2

Ingredients
1 green apple, cored and chopped
3 carrots, peeled and chopped
1 mango, peeled and stoned
7 measures/150 ml/5 fl oz freshly squeezed
orange juice, chilled
6 strawberries, hulled
slice of orange, to decorate

1 Place the apple, carrots and mango in a blender or food processor and process to a pulp.

2 Add the orange juice and strawberries and process again.

3 If liked, strain well through a sieve, pressing the juice with the back of a spoon. Discard any pulp left in the sieve.

4 Pour the drink into tumblers filled with ice cubes and serve immediately, decorated with a slice of orange.

FRUIT & GINGER ALE

An old English mulled drink, served over ice.
Roasting the fruit with cloves adds to the flavour.

Serves 4–6

Ingredients

1 cooking apple
1 orange and 1 lemon, scrubbed
20 whole cloves
7.5 cm/3 in fresh root ginger, peeled
25 g/1 oz/2 tbsp soft brown sugar
350 ml/12 fl oz/1½ cups bitter lemon or non-alcoholic wine
wedges of orange rind and whole cloves, to decorate

1 Preheat the oven to 200°C/400°F/Gas 6. Score the apple around the middle and stud the orange and lemon with cloves. Bake for 25 minutes until the fruits are soft and completely cooked.

3 Add 300 ml/10 fl oz/1¼ cups boiling water to the bowl. Using the back of a spoon, squeeze the fruit to release more flavour. Cover and leave to cool for an hour or overnight.

2 Quarter the orange and lemon and pulp the apple, discarding the skin and the core. Finely grate the ginger. Place the fruit and ginger together in a bowl with the soft brown sugar.

4 Strain into a pitcher of cracked ice and use a spoon to press out all the juices from the fruit. Add the bitter lemon or non-alcoholic wine, to taste. Decorate with orange rind and whole cloves.

VIRGIN PRAIRIE OYSTER

A superior pick-me-up and a variation on the Bloody Mary. Use only the freshest free-range eggs.

Serves 1

Ingredients

175 ml/6 fl oz/¾ cups tomato juice
10 ml/2 tsp Worcestershire sauce
5–10 ml/1–2 tsp balsamic vinegar
1 egg yolk
cayenne pepper, to taste

1 Measure the tomato juice into a large bar glass and stir over plenty of ice, until well chilled.

2 Strain the tomato juice into a tall tumbler half-filled with ice cubes.

3 Add the Worcestershire sauce and balsamic vinegar to taste and stir together well.

4 Float the egg yolk on top of the drink and lightly dust with cayenne pepper.

Variation

Shake equal quantities of grapefruit juice and tomato juice with a dash of Worcestershire sauce, strain and serve.

BLUSHING PINA COLADA

This sumptuous drink is just as good without
the rum. Make sure the ice is well crushed.

Serves 2

Ingredients

1 thick slice pineapple, peeled
1 banana, peeled, sliced and roughly chopped
3 measures/70 ml/4½ tbsp pineapple juice
1 scoop strawberry ice cream or sorbet
1 measure/22.5 ml/1½ tbsp coconut milk
30 ml/2 tbsp grenadine
pineapple wedges and maraschino cherries, to decorate

1 Cut up the pineapple
slice and add to the
blender with the banana.

2 Add the pineapple juice
to the blender and process
to a smooth purée.

3 Add the strawberry ice
cream or sorbet to the
blender with the coconut
milk and a small scoop
of finely crushed ice, and
process until smooth. Pour
into two large, well-chilled
cocktail glasses.

4 Pour the grenadine
slowly on top of the drink;
it will filter through the
drink with a dappled
effect. Decorate each
glass with a wedge of
pineapple and a cherry
and serve with drinking
straws, if liked.

Variation

For a classic Piña Colada, use vanilla ice cream
and add 1 measure white (light) rum.

ST CLEMENTS

This thirst-quenching drink confirms that freshly squeezed fruit gives a truly special flavour.

Serves 1

Ingredients

2 oranges, washed
1 lemon, washed
15 g/½ oz/1 tbsp caster sugar, or to taste
75 ml/5 tbsp water
slices of orange and lemon, to decorate

1 Pare the rind from the citrus fruits with a knife, leaving the pith. Remove and discard the pith.

2 Put the rind in a pan with the sugar and water. Heat gently, stirring, until the sugar has dissolved.

3 Away from the heat, press the rind against the sides of the pan to release the oils. Let the syrup cool. Discard the rind.

4 Purée the oranges and lemon and sweeten the fruit pulp by adding the cooled citrus syrup. Leave for 2–3 hours for the flavours to infuse.

5 Strain the pulp, pressing the solids with the back of a spoon to extract as much of the juice as possible.

6 Pour into a tall glass filled with finely crushed ice and decorate with a slice of orange and lemon.

Variation

Make soft fruit juices this way, sweetening them with sugar syrup. These will keep in the fridge for 2–3 days.

BANDREK

A rich and creamy version of the spicy Indonesian drink, to be served warm or chilled.

Serves 1

Ingredients
3 whole cloves
3 juniper berries, bruised
cinnamon stick
6 green cardamom pods, bruised
4 whole black peppercorns
1 sugar cube
175 ml/6 fl oz/¾ cup water
2 measures/45 ml/3 tbsp coconut milk
3 measures/70 ml/4½ tbsp whole milk
cinnamon sticks and a maraschino cherry, to decorate

1 Put the cloves, juniper berries, cinnamon, cardamom pods, peppercorns and sugar in a pan.

2 Heat to release the aroma and flavours. Add the water and bring the liquid to the boil.

3 Boil for 10 minutes, until reduced to 30–45 ml/2–3 tbsp of spicy flavoured syrup. Remove from the heat and cool.

4 Pour the syrup into a blender with the coconut milk and whole milk and process until smooth.

5 Strain the drink over cracked ice into a stemmed glass.

6 Decorate the glass with cinnamon sticks and a maraschino cherry.

VOLUNTEER

This pick-me-up cocktail drink was devised and drunk during a very rough sea-crossing!

Serves 1

Ingredients
2 measures/45 ml/3 tbsp lime cordial
2–3 dashes angostura bitters
7 measures/150 ml/5 fl oz chilled tonic water
decorative ice cubes, to serve
frozen slices of lime, to decorate

1 Place the lime cordial at the bottom of the glass and add the angostura bitters, according to taste.

2 Add a few decorative ice cubes to the glass, if liked.

3 Top up the glass with tonic water and add the frozen lime slices, to decorate.

Variation
Use fresh lime or grapefruit juice and a splash of sugar syrup instead of the lime cordial, and top up the glass with ginger ale.

STEEL WORKS

A thirst-quenching drink, which is ideal to serve at any time of the day or night.

Serves 1

Ingredients
2 measures/45 ml/3 tbsp passion fruit cordial
dash angostura bitters
3 measures/70 ml/4½ tbsp soda water, chilled
3 measures/70 ml/4½ tbsp lemonade, chilled
1 passion fruit (optional)

1 Pour the passion fruit cordial into a long tumbler. Add the angostura bitters to the glass and then add some ice cubes.

2 Top up the drink with the chilled soda water and lemonade and stir briefly together to mix well.

3 Cut the passion fruit in half, if using; scoop the seeds and flesh from the fruit and add to the drink. Stir the drink with a long-handled spoon before serving.

Variation
For a Rock Shandy, pour equal quantities of lemonade and soda on to bitters or use a variety of naturally flavoured and unsweetened fruit cordials.

Non-alcoholic **47**

CLASSIC & CHIC

PERFECT MANHATTAN

When making Manhattans it's a matter of preference whether you use sweet or dry vermouth, or a mixture.

Serves 1

Ingredients

2 measures/45 ml/3 tbsp rye whisky
¼ measure/5 ml/1 tsp dry French vermouth
¼ measure/5 ml/1 tsp sweet Italian vermouth
1 lemon and a maraschino cherry, to decorate

1 Pour the whisky and vermouths into a bar glass of ice. Stir well for about 30 seconds, to mix and chill.

2 Strain, on the rocks or straight up, into a chilled cocktail glass.

3 Use a canelle knife to pare a strip of lemon rind. Tie it into a knot, to help release the oils, and drop it into the cocktail.

4 To serve the drink, add a maraschino cherry with its stalk left intact.

Variation

For a Skyscraper, add a dash of angostura bitters, 5ml/ 1 tsp maraschino cherry juice, and top up with ginger ale.

Classic & Chic **49**

APRICOT BELLINI

This is a version of the famous peach-based apéritif drink served at Harry's Bar in Venice.

Serves 6–8

Ingredients
3 apricots
10 ml/3 tsp fresh lemon juice
10 ml/3 tsp sugar syrup
2 measures/45 ml/3 tbsp apricot brandy or peach schnapps
1 bottle *brut* champagne or dry sparkling wine, chilled

1 Plunge the apricots into boiling water for 2 minutes, to loosen the skins.

2 Peel off the skins of the apricots, remove the stones and discard both.

4 Add the brandy or peach schnapps to the apricot nectar and mix together.

5 Divide the apricot nectar among the chilled champagne flutes.

3 Process the apricot flesh with the lemon juice to a smooth purée. Sweeten to taste with sugar syrup, then strain.

6 Top up the glasses with the chilled champagne or sparkling wine and serve.

Variation
Instead of apricots and apricot brandy, use fresh raspberries and raspberry-infused gin or syrup.

50 Classic & Chic

DICKSON'S BLOODY MARY

This recipe has plenty of character, with the mix of horseradish, sherry and Tabasco.

Serves 1

Ingredients

2 measures/45 ml/3 tbsp vodka or chilli-flavoured vodka
1 measure/22.5 ml/1½ tbsp *fino* sherry
7 measures/150 ml/5 fl oz tomato juice
1 measure/22.5 ml/1½ tbsp lemon juice
10–15 ml/2–3 tsp Worcestershire sauce
2–3 dashes Tabasco sauce
2.5 ml/½ tsp creamed horseradish
5 ml/1 tsp celery salt
salt and ground black pepper
celery stick, stuffed green olives and cherry tomato, to decorate

1 Fill a bar glass or pitcher with cracked ice and add the vodka, sherry and tomato juice. Stir well.

2 Add the lemon juice, Worcestershire and Tabasco sauces and horseradish, to taste.

3 Add the celery salt, salt and pepper. Stir until the glass has frosted and the Bloody Mary is chilled. Strain into a long tumbler, half-filled with ice cubes.

4 Add a decorative stick of celery as a swizzle stick. Thread a cocktail stick with olives and a cherry tomato, and add to the rim of the glass, to serve.

Variation

Use tequila in the place of vodka for a Bloody Maria and mix clam juice with tomato juice for a Bloody Muddle.

LONG ISLAND ICED TEA

A long, potent drink with a highly intoxicating effect, which is well disguised by the cola.

Serves 1

Ingredients

½ measure/10 ml/2 tsp white (light) rum
½ measure/10 ml/2 tsp vodka
½ measure/10 ml/2 tsp gin
½ measure/10 ml/2 tsp Grand Marnier or Cointreau
1 measure/22.5 ml/1½ tbsp cold Earl Grey tea
juice ½ lemon
cola, chilled, to taste
slices of lemon and a large sprig of fresh mint, to decorate

1 Fill a bar glass with cracked ice and add the spirits and liqueurs.

2 Add the cold tea to the glass. Stir for 30 seconds to chill the spirits and tea.

4 Add the chilled cola, according to taste, and add a sprig of fresh mint to use as a swizzle stick.

3 Add the lemon juice, to taste. Strain the drink into a highball tumbler filled with ice cubes and the lemon slices.

Variation

For a simpler version, use equal quantities of rum, Cointreau, tequila and lemon juice and top up with cola.

HARVEY WALLBANGER

This is the next step on from a Screwdriver. Add an extra measure of vodka for a stronger version.

Serves 1

Ingredients
1 measure/22.5 ml/1½ tbsp vodka
⅔ measure/15 ml/1 tbsp Galliano
7 measures/150 ml/5 fl oz orange juice
½ small orange, to decorate

1 Pour the spirits and juice into a bar glass of ice.

2 Mix the cocktail for 30 seconds, until chilled.

4 Cut the orange slices in half and wedge them between cracked ice in a highball glass.

5 Strain the chilled cocktail into the prepared glass and serve.

3 Use a canelle knife to take strips of rind off the orange. Use a sharp knife to cut the orange evenly and thinly into slices.

Variation
Mix the orange juice and vodka with a splash of ginger wine, pour into a glass and pour the Galliano on top.

CHILLI VODKATINI

Not quite a Martini, but almost. Be sure to have your chilli vodka made well in advance and ready to use.

Serves 1

Ingredients

1 measure/22.5 ml/1½ tbsp chilli vodka
¼ measure/5 ml/1 tsp medium or dry French vermouth
2 small pickled or vodka-soaked chillies and
1 pitted green olive, to decorate

1 Add the chilli vodka to a bar glass of ice and mix for about 30 seconds, until the outside of the glass has frosted.

2 Add the vermouth to a chilled cocktail glass and swirl it round the inside, to moisten. Discard any remaining vermouth.

4 Thread the stuffed olive on to a cocktail stick, together with the pickled remaining chilli.

5 Strain the cocktail into the prepared cocktail glass. Add the olive and chilli decoration to the drink before serving.

3 Cut one of the pickled chillies in half and discard the seeds. Stuff the pitted green olive with the chilli.

Variation

For the classic Martini, use gin instead of the chilli vodka and serve with a twist of lemon.

WILGA HILL BOOMERANG

This sundowner is mixed in a large bar glass
half full of ice cubes, and is served super cold.

Serves 1

Ingredients

1 measure/22.5 ml/1½ tbsp gin
¼ measure/5ml/1 tsp dry vermouth
¼ measure/5ml/1 tsp sweet vermouth
1 measure/22.5ml/1½ tbsp clear apple juice
dash angostura bitters
2 dashes maraschino cherry juice
strip of orange rind and a maraschino cherry, to decorate

1 Pour the spirits and
apple juice into a bar glass
half-filled with ice and stir
until the glass has frosted.

2 Pour the angostura
bitters and maraschino
juice into a shorts (whisky)
tumbler. Add ice cubes.

3 Strain the mixture of gin,
vermouths and apple juice
into the shorts tumbler.

4 Add the strip of orange
rind and the maraschino
cherry and serve.

Variation

Omit the apple juice and serve the cocktail on the rocks.

Classic & Chic **55**

SINGAPORE SLING

The origins of this old-fashioned thirst quencher lie far away in the East.

Serves 1

Ingredients
2 measures/45 ml/3 tbsp gin
juice 1 lemon
5 ml/1 tsp caster sugar
soda water, chilled
⅔ measure/15 ml/1 tbsp Cointreau
⅔ measure/15 ml/1 tbsp cherry brandy
1 lemon and 1 black cherry, to decorate

1 Pour the gin into a bar glass of ice and mix with the lemon juice and sugar.

2 Strain the cocktail into a tumbler full of cracked ice.

3 Top up with soda water, to taste. Add the Cointreau and brandy but do not stir.

4 To decorate, use a vegetable peeler or sharp knife to cut a long piece of rind round the lemon.

5 Arrange the lemon rind on the glass rim. Thread the cherry on to two cocktail sticks and add to the rim of the glass to serve.

Variation
Substitute Bénédictine for Cointreau for a Straits Sling.
Swap ginger beer for soda water for a Raffles Bar Sling.

MINT JULEP

One of the oldest cocktails, this recipe originated in the south of the United States.

Serves 1

Ingredients
15 ml/1 tbsp caster sugar
8–10 fresh mint leaves
15 ml/1 tbsp hot water
2 measures/45 ml/3 tbsp bourbon or whisky

1 Place the sugar in a pestle and mortar. Tear the mint leaves into pieces and add to the sugar.

2 Bruise the mint leaves to release their flavour and colour.

4 Spoon into a snifter glass or brandy balloon and half fill with crushed ice. Add the bourbon or whisky to the snifter glass.

5 Stir well to chill. Let stand, until the ice begins to melt and dilute the drink. Serve with straws.

3 Add the hot water to the mint leaves and grind well, using a bar spoon.

Variation
Add a dash of chilled soda to the ingredients for a refreshing long drink.

KIR LETHALE

The raisins for this cocktail can be soaked overnight in vodka.

Serves 6

Ingredients
6 vodka-soaked raisins
30 ml/2 tbsp vodka or raisin vodka
3 measures/70 ml/4½ tbsp crème de cassis
1 bottle *brut* champagne or dry sparkling wine, chilled

1 Place a vodka-soaked raisin at the bottom of each glass.

2 Add a teaspoon of vodka or the vodka from the steeped raisins.

3 Divide the crème de cassis equally among the glasses.

4 When ready to serve, top up each glass with the champagne or dry sparkling wine.

Variation
For Kir Framboise, use crème de framboise or raspberry syrup and raspberry-flavoured vodka.

PLANTER'S PUNCH

This old colonial drink originates from the sugar plantations found throughout the West Indies.

Serves 1

Ingredients
1 measure/22.5ml/1½ tbsp fresh lime juice
1 measure/22.5ml/1½ tbsp orange juice (optional)
2 measures/45ml/3 tbsp dark rum
10ml/1 tsp grenadine
dash angostura bitters
soda water or lemonade, chilled
peach slices and a Cape gooseberry, to decorate

1 Squeeze the lime and orange juices and add to a bar glass of ice.

2 Add the rum and grenadine and mix together for about 20 seconds.

3 Add a dash of bitters to the bottom of a tumbler of decorative ice cubes.

4 Strain the rum and grenadine mixture into the chilled tumbler.

5 Top up with plenty of chilled soda water or lemonade and decorate with peach slices and a Cape gooseberry.

Variation
Add 1 measure/22.5ml/1½ tbsp cold Assam tea, for a different tang.

Classic & Chic **59**

KEW PIMMS

A concoction of sweet vermouth, curaçao, vodka, gin and cherry brandy served over summer fruit.

Serves 1

Ingredients

1 measure/22.5 ml/1½ tbsp sweet vermouth
1 measure/22.5 ml/1½ tbsp orange curaçao
⅔ measure/15 ml/1 tbsp vodka
⅔ measure/15 ml/1 tbsp gin
⅔ measure/15 ml/1 tbsp cherry brandy
assorted soft summer fruits
1–2 dashes angostura bitters
2 measures/45 ml/3 tbsp American dry ginger ale, chilled
2 measures/45 ml/3 tbsp lemonade, chilled
1 lemon and lemon balm or fresh mint leaves, to decorate

1 Measure the vermouth, curaçao, vodka, gin and cherry brandy into a glass of ice and stir well to chill.

2 Strain the mixture into a tall highball tumbler full of ice cubes and soft summer fruits.

3 Add the angostura bitters to the tumbler and then add equal quantities of the chilled ginger ale and lemonade.

4 Pare a piece of rind from the lemon. Cut into a rectangle and cut a slit over halfway across. Turn and repeat from the other side.

5 Twist the lemon rind to form a triangle. Add to the drink with lemon balm or mint leaves, to decorate.

STRAWBERRY DAIQUIRI

A version of the Cuban original, which was made only with local Cuban rum, lime juice and sugar.

Serves 1

Ingredients
4 whole strawberries
10 ml/2 tsp fresh lime juice
1 measure/22.5 ml/1½ tbsp brandy or strawberry brandy
1 measure/22.5 ml/1½ tbsp white (light) rum
dash of grenadine
1 strawberry and a sprig of fresh mint, to decorate

1 Place ice cubes in a clean dish towel and crush to a fine snow.

2 Process the strawberries, lime juice and brandy to a purée in a blender.

4 Pour the mixture into a well-chilled cocktail glass.

5 To decorate, replace the strawberry hull with a sprig of mint. Make a cut in the side of the strawberry and attach to the rim of the glass. Serve with a short straw, if liked.

3 Add the rum, grenadine and half a glass of ice snow to the blender and process to a slush.

Variation
For a non-alcoholic daiquiri, swap 50 ml/2 fl oz/¼ cup cream for the rum and brandy. Process in a blender and serve.

SEA DOG

A long whisky drink with a citrus twist. For a sweeter drink, add a second sugar lump.

Serves 1

Ingredients

1–2 sugar cubes
2 dashes angostura bitters
2 orange wedges
2 lemon wedges
⅔ measure/15 ml/1 tbsp whisky or Drambuie
1 measure/22.5 ml/1½ tbsp Bénédictine
2 measures/45 ml/3 tbsp soda water, chilled
maraschino cherry, to decorate

1 Place the sugar cube in a glass, add the bitters and leave to soak.

2 Add the orange and lemon wedges and press the juices from the fruit.

4 Top up the glass with chilled soda water.

5 Serve with the muddler, so that more juice can be pressed from the fruit, according to taste. Decorate the drink with a maraschino cherry.

3 Fill the glass with cracked ice. Add the spirits and mix together well.

Variation
Substitute gin for whisky and Pimms for Bénédictine.

APPLE SOUR

This variation on a Brandy Sour can be made without egg white. Use apple schnapps in place of calvados.

Serves 1

Ingredients
1 measure/22.5 ml/1½ tbsp calvados
⅔ measure/15 ml/1 tbsp lemon juice
5 ml/1 tsp caster sugar
dash angostura bitters
1 egg white
red and green apple slices and lemon juice, to decorate

1 Put the calvados, lemon juice and caster sugar into a shaker of ice, with the bitters and egg white.

2 Shake together for 30 seconds. Strain the cocktail into a tumbler of cracked ice.

3 Dip the red and green apple slices in lemon juice. Decorate the cocktail with the apple slices threaded on to a bamboo skewer.

Variation
Sours can also be made with Amaretto or tequila; add just a splash of raspberry syrup or port to the glass before serving.

INDEX